W9-ACN-286

Shakespeare's Songs

SHAKESPEARE'S
SONGS

Edited by
Alfred Harbage

*Illustrated with
the original musical
settings*

MACRAE SMITH COMPANY: *Philadelphia*

Contents

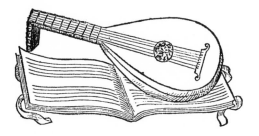

Foreword

FOR nearly four centuries Shakespeare's songs have pleased lovers of music, the theatre, and lyrical poetry. Time seems unable to stale their morning freshness. The present book brings these songs together and tries, through the illustrations, to give an idea of the kind of music to which they were originally sung. A learned introduction would here be out of place, even if the editor were capable of writing one, since those for whom the book is intended would no doubt agree with Don Pedro of *Much Ado* when his page seems more inclined to talk than to grant his request for a song: "I pray thee sing, and let me woo no more." Nevertheless, a few words of explanation may prove helpful.

All of the songs in this book are gathered from Shakespeare's plays. The playwrights and story-tellers of his time imitated actual social custom when they let their characters introduce vocal and instrumental music into their rituals and revelries, their love-making, their mourning, their moralizing—even their hawking of drygoods. When Autolycus sings of "Lawn as white as driven snow. . . . Gloves as sweet as damask roses," he is not imitating characters in modern musical comedy, but doing what a peddler of those times would really do. The difference is that the real peddler would not have hit upon phrases quite so felicitous. Thomas Dekker's "O sweet content" was written as a work song for basket-makers in a play, and his precious lullaby, "Golden slumbers kiss your eyes," for the master basket-maker when he finds himself in custody of a baby grandchild. Both songs have long outlived the play in which they first appeared.

As in so many other ways Shakespeare excelled his fellow playwrights in the number and quality of his songs. One of their wonders is that they seem so effortless, so *casual*. They never insist upon themselves in the way of show-pieces. The thought and sentiments are always simple, the language equally so. Although they must have been enjoyed for their own sake, and were intended to be, they were never dubbed in inappropriately. Scarcely any appear in the ten English chronicle plays, the three farces, and the six Greek and Roman plays where, as in the English chronicles, the action is mostly political and military. No war songs appear, perhaps because the balladry of battles long ago sufficed the English soldiery: Philip Sidney tells us that *Chevy Chase*, even when sung by some blind old fiddler, could stir his heart like a trumpet. In failing to write patriotic songs equivalent to his patriotic orations, Shakespeare missed his chance to provide his nation with its national anthem. It is in the poetic comedies, tragedies, and romances that his songs come into their own. It is no accident that the plays which seem most lyrical as a whole, *As You Like It, Twelfth Night, The Winter's Tale*, and *The Tempest*, are those which contain the most songs.

That the songs are functional—that is, fitted to the mood of the plays where they appear and to particular occasions within those plays—is usually self-evident. When the relevance of words of the lyric might be missed, I have called attention to it in the appended notes where the occasion for each song is described. These notes also contain information on sources of musical settings in those cases where there is a chance that the original tunes survive. A general word about the music must be included here since we have to remember that the songs were written to be sung just as the plays were written to be acted. The harmony of the language, which give the songs a musical quality even on the printed page, was originally matched by expressive settings and beautiful voices.

That the age of Shakespeare was musical is an historical commonplace, but few of us are fully aware of the sensitivity of the Elizabethan musical ear. In view of the swashbuckling, even primitive quality often associated with the era, the delicacy of its vocal and instrumental music is bound to come as a surprise. Volume was not prized, or at least not available, and even their "broken consorts" by mixed string and wind instruments would have seemed scarcely audible to a modern listener sitting at any distance from the performers. A single modern guitar, with its electronic amplification, would have drowned out an entire Elizabethan orchestra. The voices most enjoyed in solos were light and high, preferably soprano and countertenor, and the standards of public performance were rigidly professional. Shakespeare's company would have had its sopranos among the boys performing the parts of women and pages, and its countertenor in the "sweet-breathed fool" playing the part of a Feste or Autolycus. Among the boys the best actor was not always the best singer, and the majority of the songs were sung by attendant pages. Viola in *Twelfth Night* enters Orsino's household in the disguise of a singer, but obviously the voice of the boy filling the role proved inadequate, since the song Viola should logically sing is arbitrarily transferred to Feste, who is drafted into the scene. Guidarius and Arviragus in *Cymbeline* were obviously intended to sing their dirge for Imogen, but something must have happened to the voices of the youths filling the roles since they are provided with an excuse for reciting it instead. Fortunately the voice of the boy cast as Ariel in *The Tempest* did not change during rehearsals. Entrusting the singing so often to attendant pages was not an awkward device since in real life Renaissance ladies and gentlemen, although musically trained, did not display their talent openly except under unusual circumstances. Ophelia sings in the Danish court only after she has gone mad, and Desdemona in Cyprus only when closeted with her maid. Amiens sings in the forest of Arden even though he is the Duke's "cousin," but outlaws have their privileges.

The nature of the original settings for the songs is the subject of much debate. For the majority the original music is admittedly lost, and the earliest extant settings are by eighteenth-century composers such as Richard Leveridge, Thomas Arne, and others. (Of course there are later ones for many of the songs by such world-famous composers as Schubert, Mendelssohn, Schumann, Verdi, and their successors to the present day.) Tunes associated with certain of the songs were viewed in the late eighteenth and early nineteenth centuries as "traditional" and suggest that in these particular instances Shakespeare had written his verses to go with existing popular music. For instance, two of Ophelia's "mad" songs may originally have been sung to the widely current tune of "Walsingham," and Iago's "King Stephen was a merry peer" to a Scots tune derived from the even more widely current "Greensleeves." (That the tune of "Greensleeves" was heard at some point in the first production of some Shakespearean play seems a reasonably safe guess.) In several of the plays, notably *The Merry Wives of Windsor* and *Twelfth Night*, comic characters sing fragments of popular songs current at the time, and in some of these cases the entire songs, words and music, are known from other sources. (A single-line fragment in *The Taming of the Shrew*, "Where is the life that late I led?" has swollen, through *Kiss Me Kate*, into one of the famous bits of "Shakespeareana" of our day. Another, in *King Lear*, from a popular ballad, "Child Harold to the dark tower came," inspired a famous poem by Lord Byron.) The fragments unoriginal with Shakespeare are not collected in the present book, which limits itself to songs of at least one full stanza. One of these, "Jog on, jog on, the foot-path way," is probably not original with Shakespeare. Several of the other songs, the First Grave-digger's in *Hamlet*, and Desdemona's "Willow" song in *Othello* can scarcely be called original although the first is consciously distorted and the second slightly altered from the preexisting versions. The earlier words and music are known in both instances.

What has been said thus far may suggest that the selection of the music for the songs of Shakespeare was a fairly hit-or-miss process, but there is impressive evidence to the contrary. Most of the songs were especially written by Shakespeare for particular plays and probably provided with original musical settings. Since the dramatist was himself a lover of music and familiar with its technical terms, one is tempted to suggest that he composed some of the music himself, but there is no evidence that he did, and he may have been too diffident to invade so well-recognized a specialty. In the case of about a dozen of the songs, settings exist which we may say, with varying degrees of certainty, were those of the first performance. Associated with these settings are the names of such contemporary figures as Thomas Morley, Robert Johnson, William Byrd, John Hilton the elder, John Wilson, and Thomas Ford. Of these, Thomas Morley was the most eminent composer of Shakespeare's London, and John Wilson was destined after Shakespeare's death to become Professor of Music at Oxford. It seems not unlikely, in view of the stature of these men and the quality of the extant music itself, that the same high standards prevailed in the setting of the songs, at least the serious ones, as in the choice of singers.

Probably most of the serious songs were sung to instrumental accompaniment, even when none is indicated in the text of the plays. The instrument in most cases would have been the lute or some member of the viol family, played either by the singer himself or by a fellow performer. Even when the singing was most spontaneous and informal, as with Desdemona's "Willow" song, there could have been an off-stage accompaniment. The convention is so common, even in the theatre and cinema of to-day, that it passes without notice. In at least two instances, the serenade for Silvia in *The Two Gentlemen of Verona,* and the aubade for Imogen in *Cymbeline,* the singer or singers are accompanied by a group of musicians onstage.

It remains only to remark that in the present book those songs which are poetic in themselves or in their dramatic associations are arranged in approximately the chronological order of the plays in which they appear. In an appended section are clustered the snatches of song by comic, conniving, or drunken characters, where the literary aim was the reverse of poetic. In most of the latter cases there was probably no instrumental accompaniment. The subject of the music of the songs has been discussed by musicologists since the first half of the nineteenth century, and the issues are presented with a skill far beyond the competence of the present editor in the following recent scholarly books: John H. Long, *Shakespeare's Use of Music: A Study of the music and Its Performance in the Original Production of Seven Comedies,* 1955, and *Shakespeare's Use of Music. The Final Comedies,* 1961; Frederick W. Sternfeld, *Music in Shakespearean Tragedy,* 1963; Peter J. Seng, *The Vocal Songs in the Plays of Shakespeare, A Critical History,* 1968.

Listing by First Lines

COMIC SONGS and DRINKING SONGS

Shakespeare's Songs

I

H O is Silvia? What is she
 That all our swains commend her?
Holy, fair, and wise is she:
 The heaven such grace did lend her
That she might admirèd be.

Is she kind as she is fair?
 For beauty lives with kindness.
Love doth to her eyes repair
 To help him of his blindness,
And being helped inhabits there.

Then to Silvia let us sing
 That Silvia is excelling:
She excels each mortal thing
 Upon the dull earth dwelling.
To her let us garlands bring.

II

Spring.

When daisies pied and violets blue
  And lady-smocks all silver white
And cuckoo-buds of yellow hue
  Do paint the meadows with delight,
The cuckoo then, on every tree,
Mocks married men, for thus sings he,
  Cuckoo.
Cuckoo, cuckoo: O, word of fear,
Unpleasing to a married ear!

When shepherds pipe on oaten straws,
  And merry larks are ploughmen's clocks,
When turtles tread and rooks and daws,
  And maidens bleach their summer smocks,
The cuckoo then, on every tree,
Mocks married men, for thus sings he,
  Cuckoo.
Cuckoo, cuckoo: O, word of fear,
Unpleasing to a married ear!

I I I

Winter.

When icicles hang by the wall,
    And Dick the shepherd blows his nail,
And Tom bears logs into the hall,
    And milk comes frozen home in pail.
When blood is nipped, and ways be foul,
Then nightly sings the staring owl,
      Tu-who.
Tu-whit, tu-who: a merry note,
While greasy Joan doth keel the pot.

When all aloud the wind doth blow,
    And coughing drowns the parson's saw,
And birds sit brooding in the snow,
    And Marian's nose looks red and raw,
When roasted crabs hiss in the bowl,
Then nightly sings the staring owl,
      Tu-who.
Tu-whit, tu-who: a merry note,
While greasy Joan doth keel the pot.

IV

Fairy.

You spotted snakes with double tongue,
   Thorny hedgehogs, be not seen.
Newts and blindworms, do no wrong,
   Come not near our Fairy Queen.

CHORUS.
   Philomel, with melody
   Sing in our sweet lullaby.
Lulla, lulla, lullaby. Lulla, lulla, lullaby.
     Never harm
     Nor spell nor charm
   Come our lovely lady nigh.
   So good night, with lullaby.

FAIRY.
Weaving spiders, come not here:
   Hence, you long-legged spinners, hence!
Beetles black, approach not near.
   Worm nor snail, do no offense.

CHORUS.
   Philomel, with melody
   Sing in our sweet lullaby.
Lulla, lulla, lullaby. Lulla, lulla, lullaby. &c.

V

The
woosel cock so black of hue,
*   With orange-tawney bill,*
The throstle with his note so true
*   The wren with little quill:*

The finch, the sparrow, and the lark,
*   The plain-song cuckoo gray,*
Whose note full many a man doth mark,
*   And dares not answer nay.*

VI

Tell
me where is fancy bred,
Or in the heart or in the head?
How begot, how nourishèd?
   Reply, reply.
It is engend'red in the eyes,
With gazing fed, and fancy dies
In the cradle where it lies.
   Let us all ring fancy's knell.
   I'll begin it: Ding, dong, bell.

ALL.
   Ding, dong, bell.

Under

the greenwood tree
　　Who loves to lie with me,
And turn his merry note
　　Unto the sweet bird's throat,
Come hither, come hither, come hither.
　　Here shall he see no enemy
But winter and rough weather.

Who doth ambition shun
　　And loves to live i' th' sun,
Seeking the food he eats
　　And pleased with what he gets,
Come hither, come hither, come hither.
　　Here shall he see no enemy
But winter and rough weather.

———————

If it do come to pass
That any man turn ass,
Leaving his wealth and ease
A stubborn will to please,
Ducdame, ducdame, ducdame:
Here shall he see gross fools as he,
An if he will come to me.

VIII

Blow,

blow, thou winter wind,
Thou art not so unkind
 As man's ingratitude:
Thy tooth is not so keen
Because thou art not seen
 Although thy breath be rude.
Heigh-ho, sing heigh-ho, unto the green holly.
Most friendship is feigning, most loving mere folly:
 Then heigh-ho, the holly,
 This life is most jolly.

Freeze, freeze, thou bitter sky
That dost not bite so nigh
 As benefits forgot:
Though thou the waters warp
Thy sting is not so sharp
 As friend rememb'red not.
Heigh-ho, sing heigh-ho, unto the green holly.
Most friendship is feigning, most loving mere folly:
 Then heigh-ho, the holly,
 This life is most jolly.

Lord.

What shall he have that killed the deer?
His leather skin and horns to wear.

ALL.

Take thou no scorn to wear the horn,
It was a crest ere thou wast born,
   Thy father's father wore it,
   And thy father bore it.
The horn, the horn, the lusty horn,
Is not a thing to laugh to scorn.

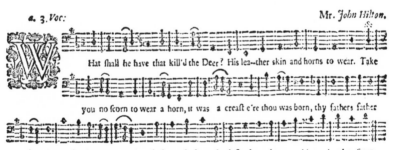

a. 3. *Voc:*   Mr. *John Hilton.*

Hat shall he have that kill'd the Deer? His lea--ther skin and horns to wear. Take

you no scorn to wear a horn, it was a creast e're thou was born, thy fathers father

bore it, and thy fa-ther wore it ; the horn, the horn, the lusty horn is not a thing to laugh to scorn.

It

was a lover and his lass,
   With a hey, and a ho, and a hey nonino,
That o'er the green cornfield did pass
   In springtime, the only pretty ringtime,
When birds do sing, hey ding a ding, ding.
Sweet lovers love the spring.

Between the acres of the rye,
   With a hey, and a ho, and a hey nonino,
These pretty country folks would lie
   In springtime, the only pretty ringtime,
When birds do sing, &c.

This carol they began that hour,
   With a hey, and a ho, and a hey nonino,
How that a life was but a flower
   In springtime, the only pretty ringtime,
When birds do sing, &c.

And therefore take the present time,
   With a hey, and a ho, and a hey nonino,
For love is crownèd with the prime
   In springtime, the only pretty ringtime,
When birds do sing, &c.

I T was a louer and his lasse, With a haye, with a hoe and a haye nonie

no and a haye nonie nonie no , That o're the green corne fields did passe in spring time. ij. ij.

the only pretting time whe birds do sing, hay ding ading ading ij. ij. sweete

louers loue the springe in spring time, ij. The onely pretiring time whe birds do sing, Haye

ding ading ading, ij. ij. sweete louers loue the spring.

Wedding

is great Juno's crown,
　　O blessèd bond of board and bed!
'Tis Hymen peoples every town,
　　High wedlock then be honorèd.
Honor, high honor, and renown
To Hymen, god of every town!

XII

Sigh *no more, ladies, sigh no more!*
  Men were deceivers ever,
One foot in sea, and one on shore,
  To one thing constant never.
    Then sigh not so,
    But let them go,
  And be you blithe and bonny,
Converting all your sounds of woe
  Into Hey nonny, nonny.

Sing no more ditties, sing no moe
  Of dumps so dull and heavy!
The fraud of men was ever so
  Since summer first was leavy.
    Then sigh not so,
    But let them go,
  And be you blithe and bonny,
Converting all your sounds of woe
  Into Hey nonny, nonny.

XIII

Pardon,

goddess of the night,
Those that slew thy virgin knight:
For the which, with songs of woe,
Round about her tomb they go.
Midnight, assist our moan,
Help us to sigh and groan
   Heavily, heavily.
Graves, yawn and yield your dead,
Till death be utterèd,
   Heavily, heavily.

XIV

O mistress

mine, where are you roaming?
O stay and hear! Your true love's coming
   That can sing both high and low.
Trip no further, pretty sweeting,
Journeys end in lovers meeting,
   Every wise man's son doth know.

What is love? 'Tis not hereafter,
Present mirth hath present laughter,
   What's to come is still unsure.
In delay there lies no plenty,
Then come kiss me, sweet and twenty,
   Youth's a stuff will not endure.

Mistresse mine.

Come

away, come away, death,
And in sad cypress let me be laid.
Fly away, fly away, breath,
I am slain by a fair cruel maid.
My shroud of white, stuck all with yew,
O, prepare it.
My part of death, no one so true
Did share it.

Not a flower, not a flower sweet,
On my black coffin let there be strown:
Not a friend, not a friend greet
My poor corpse where my bones shall be thrown.
A thousand thousand sighs to save
Lay me, O, where
Sad true lover never find my grave
To weep there.

XVI

When

that I was and a little tiny boy,
   With hey, ho, the wind and the rain,
A foolish thing was but a toy,
   For the rain it raineth every day.

But when I came to man's estate,
   With hey, ho, the wind and the rain,
'Gainst knaves and thieves men shut their gate,
   For the rain it raineth every day.

But when I came, alas, to wive,
   With hey, ho, the wind and the rain,
By swaggering could I never thrive,
   For the rain it raineth every day.

But when I came unto my beds,
   With hey, ho, the wind and the rain,
With tosspots still had drunken heads,
   For the rain it raineth every day.

A great while ago the world begun,
   With hey, ho, the wind and the rain,
But that's all one, our play is done,
   And we'll strive to please you every day.

How

should I your true-love know
 From another one?
By his cockle hat and staff
 And his sandle shoon.

He is dead and gone, lady,
 He is dead and gone:
At his head a grass-green turf,
 At his heels a stone.

White his shroud as the mountain snow,
 Larded all with sweet flowers,
Which bewept to the grave did go
 With true-love showers.

XVIII

Tomorrow

is Saint Valentine's day,
*   All in the morning betime,*
And I a maid at your window
*   To be your Valentine.*

Then up he rose and donned his clo'es
*   And dupped the chamber door,*
Let in the maid that out a maid
*   Never departed more.*

By Gis and by Saint Charity,
*   Alack and fie for shame!*
Young men will do't if they come to't,
*   By Cock they are to blame.*

Quoth she, "Before you tumbled me
*   You promised me to wed."*
"So would I ha' done by yonder sun
*   An thou hadst not come to my bed."*

XIX

And
   will 'a not come again?
   And will 'a not come again?
      No, no, he is dead,
      Go to thy deathbed,
   He will never come again.

   His beard was as white as snow,
   All flaxen was his poll.
      He is gone, he is gone,
      And we cast away moan,
   God ha' mercy on his soul!

XX

In

youth when I did love, did love,
   Methought it was very sweet
To contract the time for my behove,
   O methought there was nothing meet.

But age with his stealing steps
   Hath clawed me in his clutch,
And hath shipped me intil the land,
   As if I had never been such.

A pickaxe and a spade, a spade,
   For and a shrouding sheet:
O, a pit of clay for to be made
   For such a guest is meet.

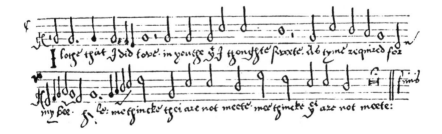

Fie

on sinful fantasy!
Fie on lust and luxury!
Lust is but a bloody fire,
Kindled with unchaste desire,
Fed in Heart whose flames aspire,
As thoughts do blow them, higher and higher.
Pinch him, fairies, mutually,
Pinch him for his villainy:
Pinch him, and burn him, and turn him about
Till candles and starlight and moonshine be out.

Take,

O take those lips away
    That so sweetly were forsworn,
And those eyes, the break of day,
    Lights that do mislead the morn:
But my kisses bring again, bring again,
Seals of love, but sealed in vain, sealed in vain.

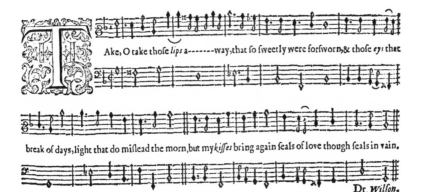

XXIII

The

poor soul sat sighing by a sycamore tree,
*   Sing all a green willow:*
Her hand on her bosom, her head on her knee,
*   Sing willow, willow, willow.*
The fresh streams ran by her and murmured her moans,
*   Sing willow, willow, willow:*
Her salt tears fell from her and soft'ned the stones,
*   Sing willow, willow, willow:*
Sing all a green willow must be my garland.

I called my love false love, but what said he then?
*   Sing willow, willow, willow:*
If I court moe women, you'll couch with moe men. . . .

The poor soule sate sighing by a Sicamore tree, Singe willo, willo, willo

wth his hand in his bosom his head vpon his knee o willo willo :||: willo O willo willo

willo willo, shall be my garland Singe all a greene willo, willo, willo willo, Aye me the

the greene willo must be my garland

He sigh'd in his singinge and made a greate moane, Singe &c
I am dede to all pleasure, my true loue she is gon, Singe &c
The mute ... ... Singe &c
His true teares fell ... ... Singe &c

Come all you forsaken and mourne you wth me, Singe &c
who speakes of a false loue, myne's falser then shee, Singe &c
Let loue no more boast her, in pallad nor bower, Singe &c
it buddds but it blasteth, ere it be a flower, Singe &c

Thou fayre more false, I dye wth thy wounde, Singe &c
thou hast lost the truest louer that goes vpon the grounde, Singe &c
Let nobdy chyde her her scornes I aprove, Singe &c
Shee was borne to be faire and I to die for loue, Singe &c

O take this for my farewell and latest adiewe, Singe &c
write this on my tombe, that in loue I was true, Singe &c

XXIV

Fools
had ne'er less grace in a year,
 For wise men are grown foppish,
And know not how their wits to wear,
 Their manners are so apish.

XXV

Then
they for sudden joy did weep,
 And I for sorrow sung,
That such a king should play bo-peep
 And go the fools among.

XXVI

He
that has and a tiny little wit,
With heigh-ho, the wind and the rain,
Must make content with his fortunes fit
Though the rain it raineth every day.

XXVII

Sleepest
or wakest thou, jolly shepherd?
Thy sheep be in the corn,
And for one blast of thy minikin mouth
Thy sheep shall take no harm.

XXVIII

Hark,

hark, the lark at heaven's gate sings,
    And Phoebus 'gins arise,
His steeds to water at those springs
    On chaliced flowers that lies,
And winking Mary-buds begin
    To ope their golden eyes.
With every thing that pretty is,
    My lady sweet, arise,
       Arise, arise!

Fear

no more the heat o' th' sun
  Nor the furious winter's rages:
Thou thy worldly task hast done,
  Home art gone and ta'en thy wages.
Golden lads and girls all must,
As chimney-sweepers, come to dust.

Fear no more the frown o' th' great,
  Thou art past the tyrant's stroke:
Care no more to clothe and eat,
  To thee the reed is as the oak.
The scepter, learning, physic, must
All follow this and come to dust.

Fear no more the lightning flash,
  Nor th' all-dreaded thunder-stone,
Fear no slander, censure rash,
  Thou hast finished joy and moan.
All lovers young, all lovers must
Consign to thee and come to dust.

No exorciser harm thee,
Nor no witchcraft charm thee.
Ghost unlaid forbear thee,
Nothing ill come near thee.
Quiet consummation have,
And renownèd be thy grave.

XXX

When
daffodils begin to peer,
*   With heigh! the doxy over the dale,*
Why then comes in the sweet o' the year,
*   For the red blood reigns in the winter's pale.*

The white sheet bleaching on the hedge,
*   With heigh! the sweet birds, O how they sing!*
Doth set my pugging tooth on edge,
*   For a quart of ale is a dish for a king.*

The lark that tirra-lyra chants,
*   With heigh! with heigh! the thrush and the jay,*
Are summer songs for me and my aunts,
*   While we lie tumbling in the hay.*

XXXI

But

shall I go mourn for that, my dear?
  The pale moon shines by night:
And when I wander here and there,
  I then do most go right.

If tinkers may have leave to live,
  And bear the sow-skin budget,
Then my account I well may give,
  And in the stocks avouch it.

XXXII

Jog

on, jog on, the foot-path way
  And merrily hent the stile-a
A merry heart goes all the way
  Your sad tires in a mile-a.

a. 3. Voc.
Mr. John Hilton.

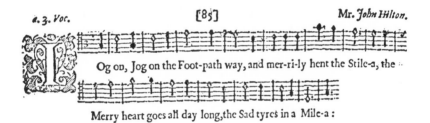

Og on, Jog on the Foot-path way, and mer-ri-ly hent the Stile-a, the

Merry heart goes all day long, the Sad tyres in a Mile-a :

XXXIII

Lawn

as white as driven snow,
Cyprus black as e'er was crow,
Gloves as sweet as damask roses,
Masks for faces and for noses,
Bugle bracelet, necklace amber,
Perfume for a lady's chamber,
Golden quoifs and stomachers
For my lads to give their dears,
Pins and poking-sticks of steel,
What maids lack from head to heel:
Come buy of me, come, come buy,
   Come buy!
Buy, lads, or else your lasses cry,
   Come buy!

Awne as white as driven Snow, Cyprese black as ere was Crow,

Gloves as sweet as Damaske Roses, Maskes for Faces and for Noses, Bugle Braceletts

Necklace Amber, Perfumes for a Ladyes Chamber, Golden Coyfes and stoma-

[65]

-chers for my Ladds, for :||: To give their Deer's Pinns and Poting sticks

Pinns :||: And poting sticks of steele what Maids lack what :||:

What :||: from head to heele, what :||:

XXXIV

Will

you buy any tape,
  Or lace for your cape,
My dainty duck, my dear-a?
  Any silk, any thread,
  Any toys for your head
Of the new'st and fin'st, fin'st wear-a?
  Come to the pedlar:
  Money's a medler
That doth utter all men's ware-a.

XXXV

Autol.

Get you hence, for I must go
Where it fits you not to know.

DORCAS.   Whither?
MOPSA.   O whither?
DORCAS.   Whither?
MOPSA.   It becomes thy oath full well
Thou to me thy secrets tell.
DORCAS.   Me too! let me go thither.

MOPSA.   Or thou goest to th' grange or mill.
If to either, thou dost ill.
AUTOL.   Neither.
DORCAS.   What neither?
AUTOL.   Neither.
DORCAS.   Thou has sworn my love to be.
MOPSA.   Thou hast sworn it more to me.
            Then whither goest? Say whither!

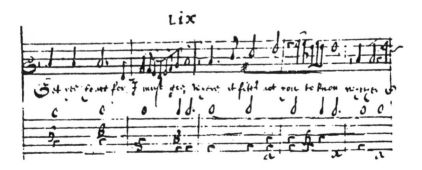

XXXVI

Full

fathom five thy father lies,
   Of his bones are coral made.
Those are pearls that were his eyes:
   Nothing of him that doth fade
But doth suffer a sea-change
Into something rich and strange.
Sea nymphs hourly ring his kneel.
                    BURDEN. Ding-dong.
Hark! now I hear them: Ding-dong bell.

Ull fathome five thy Father lyes, of his bones are Corrall made

those are pearles that were his eyes, nothing of him that doth fade but doth

suffer a Sea change into something rich and strange.

[7]

Sea Nymphs hourly ring his knell, Hark now I heare them

Ding Dong Bell Ding Dong Ding Dong Bell

Come

unto these yellow sands,
   And then take hands.
Curtsied when you have and kissed,
   The wild waves whist,
Foot it featly here and there:
And, sweet sprites, the burden bear.
  Hark, hark!
       BURDEN DISPERSEDLY. Bow, wow!
The watchdogs bark.
       BURDEN DISPERSEDLY. Bow, wow!
Hark, hark! I hear
The strain of strutting chanticleer
  Cry cock-a-diddle-dow!

XXXVIII

While
you here do snoring lie,
Open-eyed conspiracy
   His time doth take.
If of life you keep a care
Shake off slumber and beware.
   Awake! Awake!

XXXIX

Where

the bee sucks, there suck I,
In a cowslip's bell I lie:
There I couch when owls do cry.
On the bat's back I do fly
    After summer merrily.
Merrily, merrily shall I live now
Under the blossom that hangs on the bough.

XL

Juno.

Honor, riches, marriage blessing,
Long continuance, and increasing,
Hourly joys be still upon you!
Juno sings her blessings on you.

CERES.
Earth's increase, foison plenty,
Barns and garners never empty,
Vines with clust'ring bunches growing,
Plants with goodly burden bowing:
Spring come to you at the farthest
In the very end of harvest!
Scarcity and want shall shun you,
Ceres' blessing so is on you.

Orpheus

with his lute made trees
And the mountain tops that freeze
   Bow themselves when he did sing.
To his music plants and flowers
Ever sprung as sun and showers
   There had made a lasting spring.

Every thing that heard him play,
Even the billows of the sea,
   Hung their heads and then lay by.
In sweet music is such art
Killing care and grief of heart
   Fall asleep or hearing die.

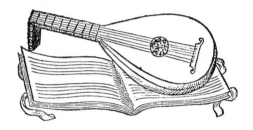

Comic Songs and
Drinking Songs

XLII

Nay,
*   by Saint Jamy,*
*   I hold you a penny,*
*   A horse and a man*
*   Is more than one*
*   And yet not many.*

XLIII

*   An old hare hoar,*
*   And an old hare hoar,*
*   Is very good meat in Lent:*
*   But a hare that is hoar*
*   Is too much for a score*
*   When it hoars ere it be spent.*

XLIV

*   Do nothing but eat and make good cheer,*
*   And praise God for the merry year,*
*   When flesh is cheap and females dear,*
*   And lusty lads roam here and there*
*   So merrily,*
*   And ever among so merrily.*

XLV

Be merry, be merry, my wife has all,
    For women are shrews, both short and tall,
'Tis merry in hall when beards wag all,
    And welcome merry Shrove-tide.

XLVI

O sweet Oliver, O brave Oliver,
    Leave me not behind thee:
But wind away. Be gone I say,
    I will not to wedding with thee.

XLVII

I am gone, sir,
    And anon, sir,
I'll be with you again,
    In a trice,
    Like to the old Vice,
Your need to sustain.
    Who with dagger of lath
    In his rage and his wrath,
Cries "Ah ha" to the devil.
    Like a mad lad,
    "Pare thy nails, dad.
Adieu, goodman devil."

XLVIII

"Was this fair face the cause," quoth she,
  "Why the Grecians sackèd Troy?
Fond done, done fond,
  Was this King Priam's joy?"
With that she sighèd as she stood,
With that she sighèd as she stood,
  And gave this sentence then:
"Among nine bad if one be good,
Among nine bad if one be good,
  There's yet one good in ten."

XLIX

Love, love, nothing but love, still love, still more,
  For, O, love's bow shoots buck and doe:
  The shaft confounds not that it wounds
But tickles still the sore.
  These lovers cry, O ho, they die!
Yet that which seems the wound to kill
  Doth turn "O ho" to "Ha, ha, he!"
So, dying, love lives still.
  O ho! a while, but Ha, ha, ha!
  O ho! groans out for Ha, ha, ha!
Heigh ho.

L

 And let me the canakin clink, clink,
 And let me the canakin clink.
  A soldier's a man,
  A life's but a span,
 Why then, let a soldier drink.

L I

 King Stephen was a worthy peer,
  His breeches cost him but a crown:
 He held 'em sixpence all too dear,
  With that he called the tailor lown.
  He was a wight of high renown,
 And thou art but of low degree:
  'Tis pride that pulls the country down,
 Then take thine auld cloak about thee.

L I I

 Come o'er the bourn, Bessy, to me . . .
  Her boat hath a leak,
  And she must not speak
 Why she dares not come over to thee.

LIII

Come, thou monarch of the vine,
Plumpy Bacchus with pink eyne!
In thy fats our cares be drowned,
With thy grapes our hairs be crowned.
Cup us till the world go round!
Cup us till the world go round!

LIV

The master, the swabber, the boatswain, and I,
  The gunner, and his mate
Loved Mall, Meg, and Marian, and Margery,
  But none of us cared for Kate.
  For she had a tongue with a tang,
  Would cry to a sailor "Go hang!"
She loved not the savor of tar nor of pitch,
Yet a tailor might scratch her where e'er she did itch.
  Then to sea, boys, and let her go hang!

LV

No more dams I'll make for fish,
  Nor fetch in firing
  At requiring,
Nor scrape trenchering, nor wash dish.
  'Ban, 'Ban, Ca-caliban
  Has a new master: get a new man.

Notes on the Songs

I.   From *The Two Gentlemen of Verona*, Act IV, Scene ii. Proteus joins Thurio and his musicians in offering a serenade to Silvia. She appears at her window and scolds him for trying to win her from his friend Valentine and for jilting his own sweetheart Julia. Julia, concealed in the shadows, hears both the song and the reproof. The latter provides immediate illustration of the virtues of Silvia stressed in the words of the song. Probably the singer was one of the company of musicians rather than Proteus or Thurio.   *swains:* young men. *inhabits:* dwells.

II & III.   From *Love's Labor's Lost*, Act V, Scene ii. These songs on spring and winter are described by Don Armado as "the dialogue that the two learned men [the curate Nathaniel and the schoolmaster Holofernes] have compiled in praise of the owl and the cuckoo" which "should have followed in the end of our show." Their show (of the Nine Worthies) has been broken up by the mockery of the ladies and gentlemen to whom the villagers offered it, and the songs serve as epilogue to the play as a whole. Their homespun quality fits well with the attack upon fashionable affectations with which the play has concluded. The ascription of the composition of the songs to Nathaniel and Holofernes suggests that they were the singers, but it seems more likely that the singers were boys. *lady-smocks:* cuckoo-flowers. *cuckoo-buds:* buttercups. *oaten straws:* musical pipes made of oat straws. *turtles:* turtle-doves. *nail:* fingernails. *keel:* skim. *saw:* moral maxim. *crabs:* crab-apples.

IV. From A *Midsummer Night's Dream*, Act II, Scene ii. The fairies, Peaseblossom, Cobweb, Moth, Mustardseed, and their companions sing this lullaby and charm as their queen, Titania, lies down to sleep in the woods. *double tongue:* fork-tongued. *Philomel:* the nightingale.

V. From A *Midsummer Night's Dream*, Act III, Scene i. Sung by Bottom to cheer himself up after his fellow-actors, frightened by his ass's head, have deserted him in the woods. *woosel:* ouzel, the English blackbird. *throstle:* song thrush. *quill:* pipe, i.e. piping voice. *Plain-song:* simple melody.

VI. From *The Merchant of Venice*, Act III, Scene ii. The death-knell of "fancy" (love based only on outward appearance) is sung, probably by a page, as Bassanio wins Portia as his bride by choosing the casket of lead in preference to those of silver and gold.

VII. From *As You Like It*, Act II, Scene v. Sung by Amiens and the other followers of the exiled Duke as they are preparing to dine in the forest. The added stanza, sung or recited by Amiens, is a parody of the song composed by the melancholy Jaques. The song expresses a major theme of the play—the respite offered man by a return to unspoiled nature. *turn:* tune. *ducdame:* a trisyllable, probably from the Welsh "dewch 'da mi," meaning "come to me."

VIII. From *As You Like It*, Act II, Scene vii. Sung by Amiens as Orlando and old Adam, who have fled from cruel brother and master, are befriended by the exiles in the forest. The theme of betrayal in the song is appropriate in view of the recent experiences of the persons assembled. *not seen:* invisible, and hence impersonal. *feigning:* pretending. *warp:* freeze.

IX. From *As You Like It*, Act IV, Scene ii. Sung by a "lord" (probably Amiens) and his companions after they have killed a deer. The music, which may have been composed by John Hilton the elder for the original production, was first published by John Hilton the younger in *Catch that Catch can*, a collection of rounds, catches, etc. issued in 1652. It is here reproduced from John Playford's *Catch that Catch can; or the Musical Companion*, edition of 1673.

X. From *As You Like It*, Act V, Scene iii. Touchstone the jester, who has been wooing the country wench Audrey, sits between two pages who sing this song of country courtship. The words, and the music scored for voice, lute, and bass viol, appear in Thomas Morley's *The First Booke of Ayres*, 1600, the only existing copy of which is in the Folger Shakespeare Library. (The illustration shows the voice part in staff notation and the lute part in tablature.) Since Morley's book appeared within a year of the original production of the play, Shakespeare and Morley may have collaborated on the song; however it is possible that the song is older than the play. *cornfield:* wheatfield. *ringtime:* time for wedding rings. *carol:* joyful song. *prime:* springtime of the year and of man's life.

XI. From *As You Like It*, Act V, Scene iv. Sung to Hymen the god of marriage as the lovers pair off at the end of the play. *Juno's crown:* Juno's crown of glory (as the wife of Jove).

XII. From *Much Ado About Nothing*, Act II, Scene iii. Sung at the bidding of Don Pedro by his attendant Balthasar as Don Pedro and Claudio are preparing to trick Benedick into falling in love with Beatrice. Benedick, who thinks he is immune, expresses disgust at Claudio's pleasure in such songs now that he has become a lover. A stage direction in the printed text of the play indicates that the part of Balthasar was taken by young "Iack Wilson," and this led to a theory, now discredited, that John Wilson was the composer of the music for the song. What may possibly have been the original tune, adapted by Thomas Ford in an arrangement for three voices, survives in a manuscript volume in Christ Church College, Oxford. *moe:* more *dumps:* sad songs, often about frustration in love.

XIII. From *Much Ado About Nothing*, Act V, Scene iii. Sung by an attendant as Don Pedro and Claudio mourn at the supposed tomb of Hero. They believe that she died of grief after they mistakenly accused her of being false to Claudio. *goddess of the night:* Diana the moon goddess, symbol of chastity. *uttered:* acknowledged.

XIV. From *Twelfth Night*, Act II, Scene iii. Sung by the clown Feste to the revelers in his mistress Olivia's household when Sir Toby Belch calls for a love song. The original tune may survive in Thomas Morley's *The First Booke of Consort Lessons*, 1599, where a tune called "O Mistresse mine" is arranged for six instruments. (The illustration shows the treble viol part as it appears in the edition of 1611.) Variations upon the tune, by William Byrd, appear in *The Fitzwilliam Virginal Book*, c. 1619, ed. J. A. Fuller-Maitland & W. B. Squire, 1894–99.

XV. From *Twelfth Night*, Act II, Scene iv. Sung by Feste when Duke Orsino, who is hopelessly in love with Olivia, asks for "that old and antique song" which "dallies with the innocence of love." The words are appropriate in view of Orsino's declared wish to find relief from love-melancholy. *cypress:* coffin of cypress-wood. *yew:* sprigs of yew, symbol of mourning.

XVI. From *Twelfth Night*, Act V, Scene i. Feste sings this whimsical autobiography after the other characters have left the stage at the end of the play. The words are nonsensical, yet melodious and strangely haunting. *When I was and:* when I was only.

XVII, XVIII & XIX. From *Hamlet*, Act IV, Scene v. Sung by Ophelia after being driven to distraction by her rejection by Prince Hamlet and the death of her father Polonius. The themes of death and frustrated desire are interwined in a way which serves almost as a diagnosis of Ophelia's mental condition. *cockle:* shell worn in the hats of pilgrims to the shrine of St. James. *shoon:* shoes. *larded:* decked. *betime:* early. *dupped:* opened. *By Gis:* old oath derived from "By Jesus." *By Cock:* old oath derived from "By God." *flaxen:* white as flax. *poll:* head.

XX. From *Hamlet*, Act V, Scene i. The First Gravedigger sings this garbled ballad on mortality (written by the Tudor poet Lord Vaux) as Prince Hamlet and Laertes watch him digging Ophelia's grave. A tune for Lord Vaux's song written for voice and lute exists in the British Museum Additional MS. 4900, ff. 62^v–63. (The voice part is shown in the illustration.) *contract:* shorten. *behove:* benefit. *meet:* fitting. *intil:* into.

XXI. From *The Merry Wives of Windsor*, Act V, Scene v. Sung by the village children disguised as fairies as they dance about the frightened Sir John Falstaff, who has been balked in his amorous attempts. *fantasy:* imaginings. *luxury:* sensuality. *bloody fire:* fire in the blood.

XXII. From *Measure for Measure*, Act IV, Scene i. Sung by her page to Mariana, who has been jilted by the Lord Angelo after their betrothal. The music, by John Wilson, survives in manuscripts and in John Playford's *Select Musicall Ayres and Dialogues*, 1652, and later books including his *The Treasury of Musick*, 1669, from which the illustration is taken. Wilson was not yet ten years old when the play was first produced but he could have used the original melody for his setting.

XXIII.   From *Othello*, Act IV, Scene iii. Sung by Desdemona as she prepares for bed on the night of her death at the hands of her jealous husband. She tells her attendant Emilia that this song of "Willow" was sung by her mother's maid Barbary who died of a broken heart, and that its refrain has been running constantly through her head. Her singing underscores the pathos of Ophelia's situation, and serves as dramatic premonition of her death. Both words and music were old at the time of the play, Shakespeare simply altering the words to fit the sex of the character. There are several early manuscript versions of the music. The illustration, a setting for voice and lute, is from British Museum Additional Manuscript 15, 117, f. 18, which belongs to approximately the time of the play.   *moe:* more.

XXIV.   From *King Lear*, Act I, Scene iv. Lear's Fool sings this complaint that masters are now taking over the role of the professional fools, thus obliquely criticizing his own master.   *grace:* favor, patronage. *foppish:* foolish. *wits to wear:* intelligence to use.

XXV.   From *King Lear*, Act I, Scene iv. The Fool's second snatch of song is less oblique in its criticism. Lear's division of his kingdom between Goneril and Regan has brought joy to these hypocrites but sorrow to the Fool, because it shows that the King has lapsed into the folly of second childhood. What may well be the original music was found by Peter J. Seng, written in the British Museum copy of *Pammelia. Musick's Miscellanie*, 1609. The words of the song are adapted from the "Ballad of John Careless," written by a Protestant martyr before his death.

XXVI.   From *King Lear*, Act III, Scene ii. Sung by the Fool after Lear has expressed his pity that the poor boy must share his own exposure to the storm. The stanza reminds us of those in Feste's concluding song in *Twelfth Night* (No. XVI), of which Shakespeare was no doubt reminded by the action in the present scene.   *and:* only.

XXVII.   From *King Lear*, Act III, Scene vi. Sung by Edgar as he continues to play the part of mad Tom o' Bedlam.   *corn:* wheat field. *minikin mouth:* delicate lips (as he plays his shepherd's pipe).

XXVIII.   From *Cymbeline*, Act II, Scene iii. Cloten, who is trying to win the favor of Imogen, commissions a band of musicians to offer this aubade (morning song) at her chamber door. The singer was probably a boy soprano in the group of musicians. What may be the original music appears with a version of the words in Bodleian MS. Don. 57, f. 78. The composer is believed to have been Robert Johnson.   *Phoebus 'gins*: the sun begins to.   *winking Mary-buds*: closed marigolds.

XXIX.   From *Cymbeline*, Act IV, Scene ii. The young princes Arviragus and Guiderius say that this dirge was sung at the burial of Euriphile, wife of Belarius, and they now alternate in reciting the first two stanzas and the lines of the third and fourth over the body of Imogen, whom they believe to be dead. Actually the final lines of adjuration seem less a fourth stanza than an addition, perhaps suggested by the conversion from singing to recitation.   *sceptre, learning, physic*: monarchs, scholars, physicians. *thunderstone*: lightning bolt.   *consign to*: join with.   *exorciser*: conjuror.

XXX.   From *The Winter's Tale*, Act IV, Scene iii. Sung by the rogue Autolycus in celebration of his life of vagrancy.   *peer*: appear. *doxy*: female vagrant. *pale*: domain. *pugging*: yearning, thieving. *aunts*: doxies.

XXXI.   From *The Winter's Tale*, Act IV, Scene iii. Autolycus's second song of defiant roguery.   *budget*: sack.   *avouch*: answer for.

XXXII.   From *The Winter's Tale*, Act IV, Scene iii. Sung by Autolycus as he takes the road to the shearing feast. The tune, probably older than Shakespeare's play, appears in *The Fitzwilliam Virginal Book* and, as set by John Hilton, in several of the music books of John Playford from 1651 onward. (The illustration is from Playford's *Catch that Catch can, or the Musical Companion*, edition of 1673.) Two additional stanzas are printed by Playford, and it is doubtful if the song was original with Shakespeare.   *hent*: cross.

XXXIII.   From *The Winter's Tale*, Act IV, Scene iv. Sung by Autolycus as he peddles his wares at the shearing feast. The music appears in John Wilson's *Cheerfull Ayres or Ballads*, 1660, and probably represents Wilson's setting of the original tune.   *Cyprus*: crape. *Bugle*: black bead.   *coifs*: caps.   *pocking sticks*: rods used for ironing ruffs.

XXXIV.   From *The Winter's Tale*, Act IV, Scene ii. Another peddler's song by Autolycus.   *toys*: trifles.   *medler*: contriver.   *utter*: bring out.

XXXV.   From *The Winter's Tale*, Act IV, Scene iv. Sung by Autolycus and the country maids who are rivals for his favor. What may be the original music by Robert Johnson was found by John Cutts in the New York Public Library MS. Drexel 4175, no. 59. (The opening bars are shown in the illustration.)   *grange*: farm.

XXXVI.   From *The Tempest*, Act I, Scene ii. Sung by the spirit Ariel, with offstage voices rendering the chime of the bell. The words confirm Ferdinand in the belief that his father has perished in the sea. The music survives in several manuscripts and in John Wilson's *Cheerful Ayres or Ballads*, 1660. In both manuscripts and book the composer is given as Robert Johnson, who was flourishing at the time of the original production of the play.

XXXVII.   From *The Tempest*, Act I, Scene ii. Sung by Ariel, with offstage voices rendering the barking of the dogs. Ferdinand is being lured toward Miranda, with whom he will fall in love at first sight.   *whist*: hushed.   *featly*: with nimble grace.

XXXVIII.   From *The Tempest*, Act II, Scene i. Sung by Ariel to awaken Gonzalo when the latter's royal master is in danger of assassination.

XXXIX.   From *The Tempest*, Act V, Scene i. Ariel sings of the life of freedom he is about to enjoy as he performs one of his final tasks by helping Prospero attire himself once more in his ducal robes. The music is preserved in a number of manuscripts and printed books, including John Playford's *Select Ayres*, 1659, and John Wilson's *Cheerful Ayres or Ballads*, 1660, where it is assigned to Robert Johnson along with the music of "Full Fathom Five."

XL.   From *The Tempest*, Act IV, Scene i. Sung by the goddesses who have come to celebrate the betrothal of Ferdinand and Miranda.   *still*: always.   *foison*: abundance.

XLI.   From *King Henry the Eighth*, Act III, Scene i. Sung by one of her maids in waiting when Queen Katherine asks for a song to relieve her melancholy. The language of the song falls short of

Shakespeare's usual felicity, and it is worth noting that it occurs in a scene of the play often attributed to John Fletcher.

XLII.   From *The Taming of the Shrew*, Act III, Scene ii. Sung by Biondello after he has described the fantastic wedding attire of Petruchio, who is approaching on horseback.   *hold:* wager.

XLIII.   From *Romeo and Juliet*, Act II, Scene iv. Sung by Mercutio to taunt the Nurse, who is acting as go-between for the young lovers. *hare hoar:* gray rabbit, used in Lenten pie.

XLIV & XLV.   From *King Henry the Fourth Part Two*, Act V, Scene iii. Sung by Silence, who has had a good deal of wine at Justice Shallow's dinner.   *shrovetide:* pre-Lenten festival season.

XLVI.   From *As You Like It*, Act III, Scene iii. Sung by Touchstone to taunt Sir Oliver Martext after Jaques has persuaded him to be married by a more respectable clergyman.   *wind:* went.

XLVII.   From *Twelfth Night*, Act IV, Scene ii. Sung by Feste after Malvolio asks him to bring writing materials so that he may tell Olivia of his confinement. By acting the part of the Vice, the Devil's agent in the old morality plays, Feste puts Malvolio in the role of the Devil.

XLVIII.   From *All's Well That Ends Well*, Act I, Scene iii. The clown Lavatch sings this jingle about Helen of Troy after the Countess has sent for Helena, her protégé.   *Fond:* foolishly. *Priam:* King of Troy.

XLIX.   From *Troilus and Cressida*, Act III, Scene i. Sung by Pandarus when Paris and Helen of Troy insist that he sing them a song of love.   *confounds:* ruins.   *not that:* not what.   *sore:* wound (also buck).

L.   From *Othello*, Act II, Scene iii. Sung by Iago after he has enticed Cassio into joining a company of drinkers.

LI.   From *Othello*, Act II, Scene iii. Sung by Iago as he succeeds in getting Cassio drunk. The latter betrays his condition by calling this foolish verse "exquisite."   *lown:* rascal.   *wight:* person.

LII. From *King Lear*, Act III, Scene vi. Edgar as Tom o' Bedlam sings the first line of an old ballad and the Fool improvises the rest of the quatrain.

LIII. From *Antony and Cleopatra*, Act II, Scene vii. The first four lines are sung by a page and the rest by the drunken guests as they dance in a ring on Pompey's barge.　　*eyne:* eyes.　*fats:* vats.

LIV. From *The Tempest*, Act II, Scene ii. Sung by the drunken butler Stephano as he stumbles upon Caliban and Trinculo cowering on the ground in fear of the storm.

LV. From *The Tempest*, Act II, Scene ii. Sung by the drunken Caliban as he revolts from Prospero and accepts Stephano as his master. *firing:* firewood.　*trenchering:* wooden plates.

Modern Scores

The following scores (except for those of "Lawn as White as Driven Snow" and "Hark, Hark, the Lark") have been condensed and edited by Paul Kauriga from Sir Frederick Bridge, *Songs from Shakespeare. The Earliest Known Settings*, London, [1894]. The composer explains in his prefatory note: "These songs I have endeavoured to present, as far as possible, in their original form and free from alterations. Where the composer has appended a figured bass, I have taken it as the groundwork of my accompaniment." The words shown in Desdemona's "Willow" song are those of the musical manuscript, without Shakespeare's alterations to fit the sex of her mother's "maid Barbary" and Desdemona herself.

IT WAS A LOVER AND HIS LASS

It was a lov-er and his lass, With a hey, and a ho, and a hey no-ni-no, and a hey — no-ni-no-ni-no.

That o'er the green corn-field did pass In spring-time, In spring-time, In spring-time, the on-ly pret-ty ring-time, When

It Was A Lover And His Lass

birds do sing, hey ding a ding, ding, hey ding a ding, ding, hey

ding a ding, ding, Sweet lov-ers love the spring, In spring-

time.   In spring-time, the on- ly pret-ty   ring-time, When

birds do sing, hey ding a ding, ding,   hey ding a ding, ding, hey

It Was A Lover And His Lass

ding a ding, ding. Sweet lov-ers love the spring.

fine

O MISTRESS MINE

O mis-tress mine, where - are you roam-ing? O mis-tress

mine where - are you roam-ing? O stay and hear! Your

- true love's com-ing, That - can sing both - high and

low. Trip - - no fur-ther, pret-ty sweet -

O Mistress Mine

ing, Jour - neys end in - lov-ers meet-ing, Ev-

- - ery wise man's son doth know. What is love? 'Tis

- not here-af-ter, What is love? 'Tis - not here-

- af-ter, Pre-sent mirth hath-pre-sent laugh-ter,

O Mistress Mine

What's to come is - still un-sure. In - - de-

lay there lies no plen - - - ty, Then - come kiss me,-

- sweet and twenty, Youth's - a stuff will not en-

dure.

TAKE O TAKE THOSE LIPS AWAY

Take, —— O take those lips —— a-

way. That so sweet-ly were for-sworn, And those eyes, the

break of day, Lights that do mis - lead the morn:

But my kis-ses bring a-gain, Seals of love, but sealed in vain.

HARK, HARK THE LARK

Hark, — — — — — — hark, hark, hark, the lark at

heaven's gate sings, — at heaven's — gate sings, And Phoebus

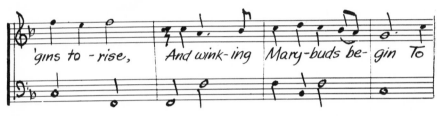

'gins to - rise, And wink-ing Mary-buds be- gin To

ope their gold-en eyes. With every thing that pretty is, My

la - dy sweet, a - rise, a - rise, a - rise! My

la - dy sweet a - rise.

O WILLO, WILLO, WILLO!

(THE POORE SOULE SATE SIGHINGE)

O wil-lo, wil-lo, wil-lo!   *pp*

wil-lo! O wil-lo, wil-lo, wil-lo, wil-lo! Shall

be my gare-land Singe all a greene

wil - lo, wil - lo, wil-lo, wil - lo!

Aye me the greene wil - lo must be my gare-land.

LAWN AS WHITE AS DRIVEN SNOW

Lawn as white as dri-ven snow, – Cypress black as e'er was crow,

Gloves as sweet as damask roses, – Masks for faces and for noses,

Bugle bracelet, necklace amber, Perfume for a la-dy's

chamber, Golden quoifs and stom-a-chers For my lads to give their

dears, Pins and poking-sticks, pins and poking-sticks, and

poking-sticks of steel, What maids lack, What maids lack, What maids

Lawn As White As Driven Snow

lack from head to heel, - What maids lack from head to heel: Come buy of me, - come, come buy, Come buy! Buy, lads, or else your lasses cry, Come buy!

FULL FATHOM FIVE

Full fa-thom five thy fath-er lies, Of his bones are co-ral made. Those are pearls that were his eyes: No-thing of him that doth fade. But doth suffer a sea - change. In-to some-thing rich and strange. Sea nymphs hour-ly ring his knell. Hark! now I hear them, Hark!

Full Fathom Five

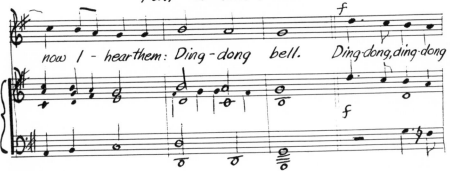

now I - hear them: Ding - dong bell. Ding-dong, ding-dong

bell. Ding-dong, ding-dong bell. Ding-dong, ding-dong

bell. Ding-dong, ding-dong bell. Ding-dong, ding-dong

bell. Ding-dong, ding-dong bell.

WHERE THE BEE SUCKS

Where the bee sucks, there suck I, ----- In a cow-slip's
bell I lie: There I couch when owls do cry. On the
bat's back I do fly Af-ter sum-mer mer-ri-ly.
Mer-ri-ly, mer-ri-ly shall I live now Un-der the blos-som that

Where The Bee Sucks

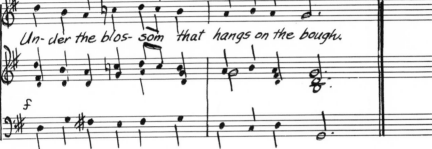

hangs on the bough. Mer-ri-ly, mer-ri-ly shall I live now

Un-der the blos-som that hangs on the bough.

First Line and Source Index